# DEATH VALLEY
## NATIONAL PARK

## SPLENDID DESOLATION

by

### STEWART AITCHISON

SIERRA PRESS
MARIPOSA, CA

# DEDICATION

To Ann and Kate—S.A.

# ACKNOWLEDGMENTS

The author and publisher wish to thank the National Park Service including Coralee "Corky" Hays, chief of interpretation, and Terry Baldino, assistant chief of interpretation, along with Charlie Callagan, Dale Housley, Mark Neuweld, and Vickie Wolfe. Special thanks also to Barbara Doram, Bill Helmer, and Pauline Esteves of the Timbisha Shoshone Village who were also helpful in providing information. Thanks, too, to Janice Newton, executive director of the Death Valley Natural History Association, and her staff. Ann Kramer and Kate Aitchison reviewed the rough draft, and Nicky Leach, editor extraordinaire, smoothed out the rough spots.

**FRONT COVER** (INSET)

Salt flats and Panamint Mountains, sundown.
PHOTO© CARR CLIFTON

**FRONT COVER/BACK COVER**

Sand dunes detail. PHOTO© DENNIS FLAHERTY

**INSIDE FRONT COVER**

Death Valley and the Black Mountains seen from Aguereberry Point. PHOTO© RANDI HIRSCHMANN

**TITLE PAGE**

Badlands and loop road through Twenty Mule Team Canyon. PHOTO© JEFF GNASS

**PAGE 4** (BELOW)

Tarantula. PHOTO© PHIL KEMBER

**PAGE 4/5**

Eureka Dunes and the Last Chance Range.
PHOTO© CARR CLIFTON

**PAGE 6/7**

Salt flats at sunrise. PHOTO© ERIC WUNROW

**PAGE 7** (LOWER RIGHT)

Palm frond detail. PHOTO © PAT O'HARA

# CONTENTS

7

# DEATH VALLEY

Date palms at Furnace Creek Ranch.    PHOTO© JEFF D. NICHOLAS

In the cool dark, I drive up the road in the Black Mountains first graded back in the 1920s to provide tourists with a startling view of Death Valley. An early advertisement had boasted, "You might enjoy a trip to Death Valley, now! It has all of the advantages of hell without the inconveniences." A common poorwill, not the devil, flushes in the headlights.

There is just a hint of day along the eastern horizon as I pull into the parking lot of Dantes View, located more than 5,000 feet high in the Black Mountains. From there, I carefully follow a primitive trail that climbs the ridge north of the parking area. The crunching of stone breaks the profound silence. Is it the movements along the great faults that created this landscape? No, just my boots hitting trail. Suddenly, a shrill trilling sends a chill up my spine. Rattlesnake! Then a flash of iridescent green and rose red sweeps by—not a snake but a broad-tailed hummingbird frantically looking for open blossoms. None here. And the hummer is gone.

A half-mile walk brings me to Dante Peak. Here I sit and wait. In the clear western sky, the pink boundary between night and day slowly descends until a snow-capped, distant peak to the northwest catches fire. That particular summit is Mount Whitney, at 14,491 feet the crown of the Sierra Nevada and the highest point in the contiguous United States. The rising sun begins to illuminate the top of Telescope Peak in the Panamint Range and reveals the yawning, shadowy graben in front of me. The bare bones of the earth are exposed, colorful, naked scarps and undulating foothills. With no trees, buildings, or familiar objects, the scale is deceptive. Badwater Basin, the lowest point in the Western Hemisphere, is an unfathomable vertical mile below me. To the south are the Avawatz and Owlhead Mountains. To the right of the Owlheads is Wingate Wash, used by some of the 1849 argonauts to escape Death Valley and later by the legendary twenty-mule team wagons. North are the Cottonwood Mountains on the west and the Grapevine and Funeral Mountains on the east side of the great valley. Behind me, backlit against the rising bright-orange sun, are the Spring Mountains over in Nevada.

I snooze but awake later hot and sweaty, cotton-mouthed and exposed skin already glowing red. Several turkey vultures teeter by me, broad dark wings held in the characteristic dihedral, drifting ever higher on a rising thermal. I move to convince them and myself that I am not dead. The sunlight hits the glistening white saltpan of Badwater. A persistent tale says that the Paiute cursed Death Valley with the name *Tomesha*, "ground afire", an appropriate name for sure, but simply a corruption of Tumbisha, the Timbisha Shoshone village at the mouth of Furnace Creek and actually closer to meaning "red ochre."

In the harsh midday light, the mountains are brooding masses of burnt iron. Most have no introductory hills, the mountains rising abruptly out of the flat, burning basin. From here, no plant life is discernible on the valley floor, but I know that on this spring morning desert gold, brown-eyed evening primrose, purple mat, and gravel ghost are in their glory.

Is that a dust devil twirling in the shimmering heat of Cottonball Basin? Do I see the long, dark line of a laboring mule team? Are those tall wagons loaded with borax looming in the haze? See the dusty figure high on the wagon box? Can I hear the rumble and chuckle of the great wheels? The creak of harnesses? The jangle of chains? The fiery voice of the teamster raised in encouragement? Do I see ghostly silhouettes of several lanky camels left over from the California-Nevada Border Survey of 1861 or the re-enactment done 121 years later? Perhaps it is the Lost Montgomery Train, a mythical horror story that grew over the decades from rumor and retelling until one version had an entire band of 400 emigrants perishing in the valley in the 1800s and their bones "scattered for miles by the coyotes and buzzards." The twenty-mule team and the bleached skeletons of lost souls are icons of Death Valley but, like so many things about the valley, it is difficult to separate the illusions, mirages, and dreams from fact.

Across the valley, I can barely make out Hanaupah Canyon, cut into the dry flank of the Panamint Range just below Telescope Peak. That's where one dreamer, Alexander "Shorty" Borden, hand-built a 10-mile road to his lead and silver diggings back in the 1930s. Like

---

**OPPOSITE:** *Mesquite Flat Dunes and Amargosa Range, early morning.* PHOTO© CHARLES GURCHE

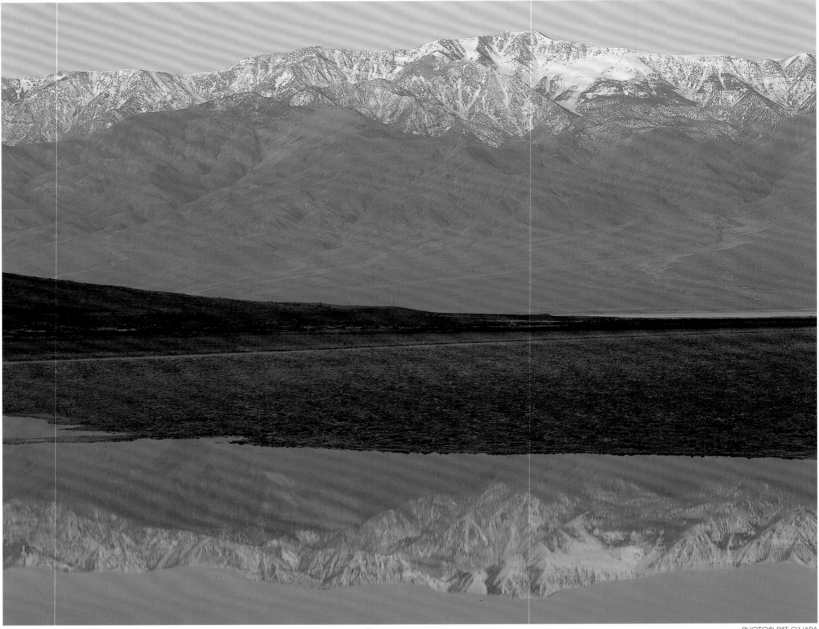

Snow-covered Telescope Peak and Panamint Mountains reflected in the pool at Badwater.

so many of the mining ventures in the area, the cost to transport the ore to a smelter proved more than the ore was worth. Shorty eventually abandoned mining and lived off handouts from passing tourists. Today, the flowing sweet stream lined with willow, mesquite, and wild grape masks the lost dreams of the old prospector and beguiles the hiker who climbs into this canyon sanctuary.

I take a sip of warm water from my canteen and retreat down the mountain to my air-conditioned car. I'll cook if I wait here for late afternoon, when long golden rays of sunshine will turn the mountains into radiant ships on a calm sea. Dantes View…indeed.

Devils Cornfield.

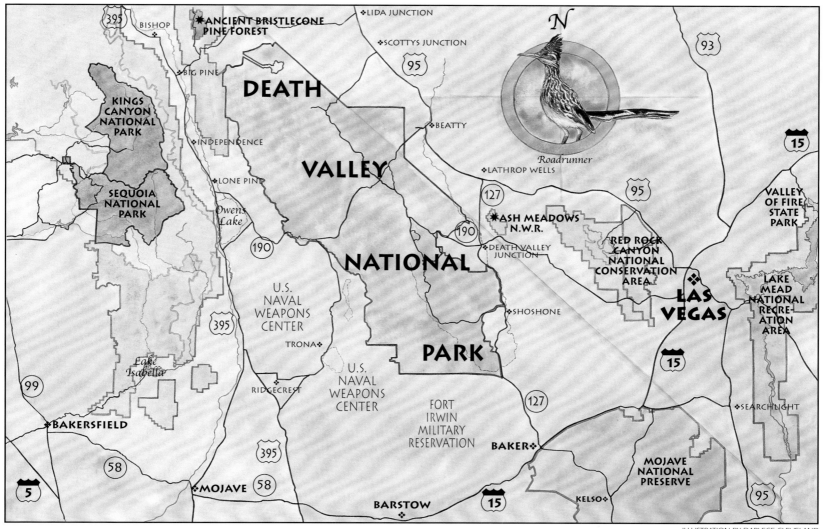

ILLUSTRATION BY DARLECE CLEVELAND

Death Valley National Park is a land of sailing rocks, musical dunes, sublime vistas, and tall tales. Let's look at some of the dry facts: ecologically, Death Valley lies within the very northern part of the Mojave Desert and is also part of the Great Basin, a region covering much of the intermountain West. In the Great Basin rivers and streams do not flow out to an ocean but into valleys or basins where the water sinks, evaporates, and/or becomes a saline lake. Death Valley and its surrounding mountain ranges are also within the geologic province called the Basin and Range, where stretching and large-scale faulting of the earth's crust has produced a series of roughly parallel, north-south–trending valleys and ranges.

By the 1920s, Death Valley's scenic wonders were becoming known to the outside world, and some mine operators thought that there might be more gold in the pockets of tourists than in the rocks of Death Valley. One former borax mining company employee, Stephen Mather, became the first director of the National Park Service and a strong promoter of setting the valley aside as a national park. Furthermore, popular books and articles in the *Saturday Evening Post* boosted visitation, and on September 30, 1930, a new radio show called, *"Death Valley Days"* aired. Mather's successor as park service director, Horace Albright, convinced President Herbert Hoover to sign an executive order temporarily withdrawing Death Valley from further exploitation. During his last days in office in 1933, Hoover signed the proclamation establishing 1,600,000 acres as Death Valley National Monument.

Fifty years later, when the Mojave and Colorado Deserts Biosphere Reserve was designated, the national monument was included. However, conservationists and scientists still worried that not enough of southern California's desert ecosystem was being preserved. In 1994, Congress passed the Desert Protection Act, which enlarged the monument area to more than 3,396,000 acres, an area greater than the state of Connecticut, and changed its status from national monument to national park. Death Valley National Park is now the largest national park in the lower 48 states. Although more than three million of these acres are currently managed as wilderness, many miles of roads (albeit, of varying quality) allow access to the far corners of the park. Today's park takes in not only Death Valley but also Saline Valley, Eureka Valley, a substantial part of the Panamint Valley, and, of course, the many intervening mountain ranges.

L.F. Noble, a pioneering Death Valley geologist, studied the jumbled rocks of the Virgin Spring area in the Black Mountains in the 1930s. He found this region so complexly faulted and folded, that he named it the "Amargosa Chaos." The geologic history of Death Valley is one of deposition, crustal stretching and deformation, and erosion; and while geologists have come to know well the characters starring in this geologic story, the many subplots have yet to be revealed and understood.

Geologic history is divided into four great chapters, or eras, loosely based on the dominant life forms during each period. Much of the bedrock in Death Valley's mountain ranges is made of Precambrian-age material, a time when life on earth consisted of single-celled organisms like bacteria. Marine sediments deposited 1.8 billion years ago were later transformed by heat into metamorphic rocks during mountain-building episodes. These primal mountains were then worn down before the end of the Precambrian, some 570 million years ago.

During the next geologic era, the Paleozoic, the entire west coast of North America was a quiet continental shelf. In this warm, tropical, (tropical because North America was centered on the equator at this time due to plate movement— but that's another story) shallow sea, life was abundant. Clams, snails, sea stars, urchins, sea lilies, trilobites, brachiopods, corals, and bryozoans populated the ocean. A steady "rain" of shell fragments mixed with sand, silt, and clay washed in from shore fell on the ocean floor, accumulating there at a slow average rate of one one-thousandth of an inch per year. Yet after 350 million years, more than 20,000 feet of sediment had been deposited. Most of

the exposed rock layers in Death Valley are from this era.

Starting in the Late Paleozoic (and continuing into the next era), the Death Valley landscape changed dramatically. To the west, the Pacific Ocean floor (a tectonic plate) began to dive under (a process geologists call subduction) the western edge of the North

American continent (another tectonic plate). Increasing temperatures at greater depths melted rocks, and the hot magma bubbled toward the surface. Where the magma cooled underground, granite was crystallized. Where the molten material erupted onto the surface, volcanoes, ash, and lava flows produced a landscape resembling the present-day Cascade Range. Deposits of gold, lead, silver, zinc, and copper were injected. Compression forced huge blocks of rock to slide horizontally (thrust faulting), superimposing the sequences of the Paleozoic sedimentary forma-

tions on top of one another. The region was no longer coastal real estate, as it had been for the previous billion years.

The Paleozoic Era concluded with "the Great Dying," a vast extinction of marine (about 90 percent of the species) and terrestrial (about 70 percent) organisms. Recent evidence suggests a large meteor collided with the earth, abruptly changing the climate and possibly initiating violent volcanic eruptions.

While this mountain-building episode was occurring, dinosaurs were becoming the rulers of the Mesozoic earth. However in the park area, there was little dry land except for the slopes of active volcanoes. This lack of appropriate habitat probably accounts for the relative absence of dinosaur fossils in the park. Much of the volcanic material has since been eroded away.

Like the Paleozoic, the Mesozoic Era also ended with a bang about 65 million years ago. Another large meteor crashed into earth, altering the climate, and wiping out the dinosaurs. As the dust settled, the Cenozoic Era was ushered in. Eventually, in the American West, the earth's crust began to be stretched, great parallel faults formed, and the blocks of crust between faults became unsteady and rotated. Mountains were uplifted and valleys down-faulted. This was the genesis of today's Basin and Range landscape.

Death Valley is just one of these basins and began to form within the last three million years. Over that time, the amount of offset between the huge blocks of earth's crust is truly staggering. For instance, in the Badwater Basin, the bedrock is covered by more than 9,000 feet of material from the surrounding mountains and mixed with salts from past lakes. The summit of Telescope Peak is more

**ABOVE:** Polished walls of Mosaic Canyon. PHOTO© GLENN VAN NIMWEGEN

than 11,000 feet high, so the total vertical offset has been at least 20,000 feet! Furthermore, there has been horizontal movement along some of the faults, occasionally in excess of 50 miles.

Beginning about 28 million years ago, another series of Promethean eruptions covered the region with more than 1,000 feet of volcanic ash. Lava flows and ash beds dating from between 12 and 4 million years ago lie within the Black Mountains, Saline Range, and Argus Mountains. Even younger are the cinder cones in southern Death Valley and Saline Valley. Ubehebe Crater and its neighboring volcanic features are practically fresh, at a mere 3,000 years of age (new findings suggest the crater may be only 300 years old).

In Death Valley, Lake Manly filled until it was more than 600 feet deep, eight miles wide, and 90 miles long. Up to 25 horizontal terraces, called strandlines, cut into Shoreline Butte and elsewhere in the valley, and indicate Lake Manly stabilized for a long time at a particular level. Wind-generated waves pounding on the shore carved these terraces. How-

With the lack of precipitation, there is little soil development. Without soil, when the rains do come, they have nothing to soak into. The water sheets off the barren slopes into small drainages, which feed into larger ones, and a flashflood is born. Sand, cobbles, and boulders are washed downstream, carving a deeper canyon into the mountainside. When the flood exits at the canyon's mouth, the debris (alluvium) and water spread out into a fan shape and come to rest. Death Valley is world famous for the incredible size, shape, and exposure of these alluvial fans. Fans grow and may merge with neighboring fans to form a broad gently sloping pediment surface on the valley floor. Future floods can add to this accumulation of sediment

During the Pleistocene, a subdivision of the Cenozoic lasting roughly from 2 million to 10,000 years ago, the climate was much cooler and wetter than today. Woodlands of pinyon, juniper, and scrub oak extended nearly to the valley floor. Mastodons, horses, camels, sloths, antelope, and some of the larger cats roamed the area. Their fossil tracks are occasionally found at places like Salt Creek Hills, south of the Devils Cornfield. Glaciers accumulated in the Sierra Nevada and other high mountains, and rivers flowed into the valleys.

ever, by 10,500 years ago, the end of the last ice age, Lake Manly was totally dry.

For the last 10,000 years, the Death Valley area has become increasingly sere, but there have been relatively brief respites from that trend. For example, from about 5,000 to 2,000 years ago, wetter weather allowed another lake, albeit considerably smaller than Manly, to form in Death Valley. The evaporation of this body of water left the upper layer of salts we see today covering the valley floor.

Paradoxically, water is one of the major creators and sculptors of desert landscapes.

or cut new drainages into it. The ever-present desert wind helps to polish and shape the landscape, too, but not nearly as aggressively as moving water. At the higher elevations, freezing water wedges rocks apart and adds to the erosional process.

Nineteenth-century geologist G.K. Gilbert commented that the geology of Death Valley is "beautifully delineated on the slopes of the distant mountains, revealing at a glance relations that in a fertile country would appear only as the results of extended and laborious investigations." Wouldn't he be surprised.

**ABOVE:** Fossil ammonites exposed in the walls of Bighorn Gulch. PHOTO© JIM STIMSON

# HUMAN HISTORY

People have lived in or passed through Death Valley for more than 10,000 years. The earliest known people, the Nevares Spring Culture, hunted with spears and spear throwers known as atlatls for mastodons, horses, camels, ground sloths, pronghorn antelope, and large cats along the shore of Pleistocene Lake Manly. They gathered stones into circles to support brush shelters and dug pits to store food. Over a couple of millennia, the climate became hot and dry, hotter than today. Lake Manly evaporated, vegetation died, the larger animals left, and the people probably avoided the valley.

Then, about 5,000 years ago, the climate moderated to a wetter, cooler period, and a new but smaller lake formed and hunters returned. Known as the Mesquite Flat Culture, these people were similar to earlier hunters and gatherers in that they, too, built brush shelters and fashioned stone tools. Mortars and pestles were used to grind seeds, and insects were an important source of protein. Over the centuries, another warming trend dried this lake and the Mesquite Flat people drifted elsewhere.

By A.D. 500 climatic conditions in Death Valley were similar to today, but a new group of hunters and gatherers, the Saratoga Springs Culture, armed with bows and arrows, were attracted to the area. Big game was scarce so these people relied more on plant foods. They used portable millstones rather than mortars to grind seeds. They crafted ceramic bowls, water jugs, cooking pots, and clay figurines for use in religious ceremonies. They traded with their neighbors, acquiring painted bowls from the people of the Colorado Plateau; seashell beads, carved schist pendants, and bright parrot feathers from Mexico; and seashells from the West Coast. They pecked petroglyphs and painted pictographs on the rocks, and constructed geoglyphs, which are large-scale figures created by aligning certain rocks and removing others to expose the lighter colored soil beneath. Often geoglyphs can only be appreciated from an aerial vantage point.

Over time, the Saratoga Springs people probably mixed with other incoming groups. By about 1,000 years ago, a new culture in Death Valley had emerged: the Timbisha Shoshone. They made a distinctive type of arrowhead, pottery, and baskets. They stored mesquite beans, one of their main foods, and other plant items in pits and used grinding stones, or metates, and handstones, or manos, as well as wooden mortars for grinding seeds. During the winter, they lived in roofless brush shelters or conical log dwellings. When summer temperatures soared, the people retreated to the mountains. Surrounding the Timbisha were other native groups: the Northern Paiute, the Ute, Chemehuevi, Kawaiisu, and Coso cultures.

The first documented non-Indians in the Death Valley area were led by an enterprising Spanish horse trader from Santa Fe, New Mexico, Antonio Armijo. Enroute from New Mexico to California, his caravan reached the Amargosa River, south of the Spring Mountains, on January 14, 1830. They followed the river into the extreme southern end of Death Valley, then continued south, going around the Avawatz Mountains to Bitter Spring, eventually reaching the San Gabriel Mission. A month later, Armijo returned with a herd of horses that would sell for five times what he had paid.

Fourteen years after Armijo, U. S. Army Captain John C. Fremont followed the same

**ABOVE:** Pictographs in the Greenwater Range. PHOTO© FRED HIRSCHMANN

trail. He paused at Salt Spring, where the trail crossed a braided stream, and remarked, "a very poor camping place…with very little unwholesome grass. The water is entirely too salty to drink." He also noted, "It (the river) is called by the Spaniards Amargosa—the bitter water of the desert." His 1844 route became known as the Old Spanish Trail although primarily Indians, Mexicans, and later American pioneers used it.

During the fall of 1853, Lieutenant Tredwell Moore led a party of surveyors to the Death Valley region to locate a railroad route over the Sierra Nevada and through eastern California. The expedition failed in its primary mission, but information gathered led to the publication of the first map of the northern Death Valley area in 1857. Although other surveyors skirted and occasionally passed through Death Valley, it was the U.S. Army Corps of Engineers George M. Wheeler whose extensive topographic and scientific surveys of the West in the 1870s brought to light the area's fascinating archaeology, geology, botany, and zoology. Wheeler's men also drafted accurate topographic maps of the region.

A few years later, in 1874, Andrew Jackson Laswell and Cal Mowrey became the first white settlers in Death Valley. They developed farms at Bennett's Well and Furnace Creek to supply alfalfa and other crops to mining towns in the Panamint Mountains.

In 1891 the U.S. Department of Agriculture's Death Valley Expedition, first in a series of biological surveys of the West conducted by Clinton Hart Merriam, chief of the department's Division of Ornithology and Mammalogy, explored the area. Merriam was continuing his study of the distribution of plants and animals, which would be used to assess the suitability of western lands for farming and ranching. Expedition botanist Frederick Vernon Colville wrote the report, *Botany of the Death Valley Expedition*, considered a classic in field ecology. Also along were George Bird Grinnell, T.S. Palmer, and Vernon Bailey. The expedition was a veritable who's who of the first American ecologists.

For the next couple of decades, Death Val

ley continued to be the harsh, intimidating abode of the grizzled prospector, hardy explorer, and a few Indians. Then in 1907, part of the course for the Great Automobile Race, an around-the-world-race sponsored by the *New York Times* and the Paris newspaper *Le Matin*, passed through Death Valley. This event altered the way the American public would view this obscure place forever. Soon auto manufacturers were featuring Death Valley in their sales promotions and tourists were venturing into the desert, and everywhere else, in their new-fangled vehicles.

A couple of years later, the U.S. Geological Survey issued a guide by geologist Walter C. Mendenhall to the "watering places" throughout the eastern California-southern Nevada desert country, which would prove to be handy for visiting Death Valley. He also offered some sage advice about desert travel: "Carry pick, shovel, bucket, and rope. Take a heavy overcoat and blanket. Wear a broad-brimmed gray felt hat and stout hobnailed boots. And don't cut your hair too short."

In January 1919, western writer Zane Grey came for a visit and was inspired to write another novel. Two years later, the intrepid Edna Brush Perkins and Charlotte Jordan became the first women to explore Death Valley on their own. Movie cameras arrived in 1923 and 1924 to film parts of Grey's *Wanderer of the Wasteland*. The horse opera was Hollywood's first all-color film and an instant box office hit.

As mining ventures slacked off, the business of tourism was gaining momentum. One of the first tourist camps was a collection of tent houses near Stovepipe Wells. Then a borax company converted some of their buildings into the Furnace Creek Ranch. Several miles away, the swank Furnace Creek Inn, an adobe-and-native-stone hotel designed by Los Angeles architect Albert Martin and paid for by the Pacific Coast Borax Company, opened in 1927. In a few years a swimming pool, tennis courts, golf course, and airfield were added to keep up with an explosion of tourism in the valley.

Zane Grey predicted Death Valley would "never be popular with men" and was "fatal to women," but visitation now approaches one and a half million people per year. Europeans account for the majority of summer visitors, apparently, wanting to experience the true, brutal desert at its best, or worst!

**ABOVE:** Abandoned talc mine in the Ibex Hills. PHOTO© FRED HIRSCHMANN

Death Valley, late afternoon view from Dantes View. PHOTO© PHIL KEMBER

# A LAND of EXTREMES

Death Valley National Park can be summed up in one word: extreme. Death Valley is the hottest, lowest, and driest place in the United States. The record high temperature was a scorching 134° F on July 10, 1913. Understand that official temperatures are measured in the shade three feet off the ground! Azizia, Libya holds the world record for sizzle: 136° F. However, Azizia's average daily July maximum is a relatively cool 99° F compared to Death Valley's 116° F.

Death Valley's hottest "unofficial" temperature was 201° F measured on the ground in direct sunlight. By contrast, winter nights can be quite cool. The coldest temperature recorded at Furnace Creek Ranch was 15° F, surprisingly also in 1913. January's average daily minimum is 39° F. Of course, the higher mountains surrounding the valley experience much colder temperatures and may receive several feet of snow during the winter. Incidentally, Furnace Creek was not named for the summer's heat but rather refers to a little stone furnace built by Asabel Bennett in 1860 to test ore samples for silver.

Badwater Basin, baptized by a surveyor after his thirsty burro refused to drink, is the lowest spot in the Western Hemisphere. The exact lowest spot is 282 feet below sea level and about 3.3 treacherous miles west of the roadside parking area, which is only a few feet higher. Legend wrongly claims that the water contains arsenic, but the emetic water does have Glauber's salt, gypsum, trona, and table salt. No wonder the burro wouldn't drink. Amazingly, a tiny endemic snail survives in the briny pools. Eighteen miles across the valley, Telescope Peak rises to 11,049 feet, giving the distance between the valley floor and the mountain summit the sharpest vertical rise found in any U.S. national park. Yet, Badwater is still 1,030 feet higher than the world's lowest spot, the Dead Sea.

Death Valley is the driest place in North America. The relative humidity can be as low as 3 percent. Furnace Creek, near the center of the valley, averages 1.9 inches of precipitation annually. The wettest month is February, which may receive about one-third of an inch; the driest is June, which averages 0.03 inches. Keep in mind that these are averages. In 1929, and again in 1953, not a single drop of rain was recorded. By contrast, more than six inches fell during the winter of 1997-98. Along with low precipitation is a very high evaporation rate—150 inches per year. A 12-foot-deep lake, with no other source of water, would dry up in a year! However, the driest place in the world is Arica, a small village in the Atacama Desert of Chile, which averages a mere 0.03 inches of precipitation per year. to learn that even after more than a century of study, geologists are still puzzling over many of Death Valley's features?

# Of Mules and Men

The Clock Tower at Scottys Castle.            PHOTO© LARRY ULRICH

Sometimes I imagine myself as one of those old, crusty, sun-baked, grizzled prospectors, a couple of fuzzy-eared burros trailing behind. Loaded in the panniers, I have pinto beans and sourdough starter, plenty of flour, some Arbuckle coffee, sugar, canned tomatoes, and a slab of bacon. I also have a small bag of raw oatmeal, not for breakfast, but a few flakes to put in my canteen to neutralize the alkalinity of desert spring water. My prize possession is a black, iron Dutch oven that will bake biscuits or fry meat or boil beans, even make camp coffee. Several metal cans store my precious water. There is also a gold pan, a little vial of mercury for amalgamating any finds, a rock hammer, and a well-thumbed Bible. A tarp strapped across the top of the load doubles as my tent and shade. Inside the tarp is an old Navajo chief's blanket. Should serve. Won't get too cold at night anyway. The shovel tied on one side and a pick on the other rounds out my prospecting kit.

With such a heavy load, it's really no surprise that my burros have sad, brown eyes and an ornery disposition. But I'm off into the Valley of Death to search for El Dorado. I know it's out there somewhere. After all, one of the Jayhawkers supposedly found an intriguing black rock high on Tucki Mountain. Later he had a gunsmith fashion it into a gunsight, who recognized the ore as silver. Many returned to Death Valley searching for the Lost Gunsight Lode. Even Manly, who led the Bennetts and Arcans out of Death Valley, was lured back 11 years later to look for the Lost Goller, but to no avail. And wasn't it in 1864 that Jacob Breyfogle was found on the Old Spanish Trail raving about hostile Indians and gold-laced quartz crystals in his pockets? Sure no one else has ever found the Lost Breyfogle Mine…yet. All it takes to get rich, though, is a grubstake and a little luck…well, maybe a lot of luck.

The first real producing mine in the Death Valley area was the Christmas Gift. A deposit of antimony sulphide and a little silver was discovered in Nemo Canyon on the west of the Panamints on Christmas Day, 1860. After the big strike at Panamint City in 1873, the Death Valley region witnessed a series of boom-and-bust mining camps as prospectors swarmed over the area. Chloride City, Keane Wonder, Bullfrog and Rhyolite, Greenwater, Harrisburg and Skidoo,

and Ashford Mill to the Leadfield swindle of 1926—all broken dreams of those who thought wealth could be easily wrestled from the desert rock.

But the lure of gold and silver drew men (and a few women) to scratch the desert to satisfy their itch for wealth. Why yes, back in 1905, Lillian Malcolm came down in the valley to prospect with three men. That caused a few eyebrows to lift in Rhyolite, but what really got a reporter goin' was that Lillian left in "masculine dress." In other words, she dared to wear pants!

Colorful schemes that sounded good late at night over the dying embers of a campfire and with a few whiskeys warming the belly often bleached out in the harsh light of the next day. Some of those early dreamers and schemers died in their pursuit—occasionally violently at the hands of rival prospectors or displaced Indians. Some died from exhaustion, starvation, or dehydration. And then there's the tale of a traveler crossing a soft, boggy part of the saltpan and discovering a dead man's face peering up at him from the brilliant ground. "He was a Swede with yellow hair, and he stared at the sun. He had sunk standing up." Truth or desert madness? Back in 1886, mule teamster Al Bryson was killed by his swamper Sterling Wassam with a shovel after an argument over a dull can opener. Too much desert sun?

Only a very few found anything of material value. Some discovered personal things about themselves, and some loved the search and the end result was of little consequence. Frank "Shorty" Harris, a self-described single blanket jackass prospector who sold what would become the fabulous Bullfrog Strike for a paltry sum while drunk, once said, "Who the hell wants $10,000,000?" It's the game, man—the game."

Clues in the rock. I search for breaks in the rock faces where white intrusions of quartz-rich veins may have brought up gold. During my trek along the central valley floor, I come across nearly 100 stone mounds. Some sort of mining cairns? No, archaeologists have studied the mounds, which range in size from eight to 18 feet in diameter and up to three feet in height, and determined that a few are Indian burials but most serve an unknown purpose. Over in

"Cowboy Register" in the Nelson Range.

Marble Canyon, while scanning the walls, I find petroglyphs pecked into the stone. A pregnant bighorn, lizards, and birds, along with abstract drawings are depicted, but no carved maps leading to lost mines. In the canyons where Paleozoic limestones, dolomites, and shales are exposed, exquisite fossils of trilobites, sea lilies, horn coral, and brachiopods hint at the diversity of life eons ago, but no clues to mineral wealth. The yellow gold eludes me.

If it doesn't work out, if I don't hit the "Mother Lode," well, I can set up a little shack, fill it with old salvaged mining equipment, mineral specimens, bottles colored purple by the sun, and Indian relics and call it a trading post and have tourists take pictures of me just like Burro Bill Price and his wife Edna did back in 1931 at Salt Creek Crossing. Only problem is all these historic artifacts are protected and treasured by scientists and visitors, so I'd better leave them alone. But somewhere, beyond the horizon, the mother lode is out there…just awaitin'.

Cashier Mill at Harrisburg, sunset.

Mesquite Flat Dunes and the Cottonwood Mountains.

PHOTO© JEFF D. NICHOLAS

# The BENNETT-ARCAN PARTY

The Bennett and Arcan families had been waiting anxiously at the spring for almost four weeks for the return of William Manly and John Rogers. Their food was virtually gone. The other families and single men had left the camp days or weeks before and had not returned. Had they made it out of the valley? Or did they die trying?

Gold was discovered on the eastern slopes of the Sierra Nevada in 1848, and by the following year hordes of hopeful argonauts were on their way west. One group of about 500 Forty-niners arrived in Salt Lake City in October 1849. It was too late in the year to go directly west from Salt Lake. Several years prior, the Donner Party had attempted to do just that, but many had died in the snowbound mountains, and those who did survive had been forced to resort to cannibalism.

One hope, though, was the Old Spanish Trail, a route roughly approximated by today's Interstate 15, southwest from Salt Lake City. Although no wagon trains had ever traversed this route, it did bypass the high Sierras. The Forty-niners set out on this trail, but travel was slower than expected. One day, a party of packers rode into camp with a crude map showing a westerly shortcut across the desert. Most of the 120 wagons decided to follow the cutoff. The others would continue along the Spanish Trail.

The "shortcut" almost immediately ran into a precipitous canyon with endless desert beyond. All but 20 wagons returned to the Spanish Trail. Once across the canyon, disputes arose about which way to go, and the group splintered into smaller factions.

Some abandoned their wagons, packed food, water, and belongings in sacks and began walking. They were never seen again. The remaining wagons rolled slowly westward. One group, the "Jayhawkers," descended Furnace Creek Wash to Travertine Springs, arriving on Christmas Eve. Although their thirst was slaked by the water here, ahead were horrible salt flats, and beyond rose what appeared to be an impenetrable wall of mountains.

At the edge of the Mesquite Dunes, they slaughtered several oxen and used the wood from their wagons to build fires to dry the meat into jerky. On foot, these '49ers climbed toward Towne Pass then turned south over Emigrant Pass into Wildrose Canyon and escaped the valley.

Two days after Christmas, the Bennett, Arcan, and Wade families, along with an assortment of stragglers, arrived at the mouth of Furnace Creek. Refusing to abandon their wagons, they decided to head south down Death Valley, hoping to find a pass through the Panamint Range.

Near the spring now known as Bennett's Well came another split in the party. The Bennetts, Arcans, and some of the singles would stay here while two of the younger men, Manly and Rogers, would search for a route over the mountains and get help. The Wades and their companions decided to continue south in hopes of crossing the Spanish Trail.

As the weeks passed, some of the people left behind became restless and set off on their own. After one day, one of them, Richard Culverwell, realized he was too weak and turned around, but he never made it back to camp. The very next day, February 8, Manly and Rogers returned and rescued the remaining families. Legend has it that as Manly, Bennett, and Arcan crested the Panamint Range, they looked back and cursed the place with the words, "Goodbye, Death Valley!"

Traditional Shoshone dwelling of the Death Valley area, 1935.

PHOTO BY GEORGE GRANT, COURTESY NATIONAL PARK SERVICE, DEATH VALLEY NATIONAL PARK

# THE TIMBISHA SHOSHONE

Even as the last of the '49ers struggled out of Death Valley, the first prospectors were on their way to the valley, where they, of course, encountered native people. Various subgroups of the Western Shoshone were living in the area, migrating seasonally to harvest wild plants and hunt rabbits, rodents, birds, reptiles, and bighorn sheep. Extended family groups would establish camps at the few reliable water sources. During the winter, the Shoshone would live at the lower elevations in roofless brush shelters or conical log dwellings.

Unfortunately, the continuing influx of "outsiders" eventually disrupted the self-sufficient lifestyle of the natives and hostilities flared. The Treaty of Ruby Valley was signed in 1863, and many Western Shoshone abandoned their traditional life and took up jobs such as guides, miners, woodchoppers, domestic helpers, and ranch hands.

During the late 1920s and early 1930s, the Timbisha subgroup of the Western Shoshone lived in four different locations in the Furnace Creek area. In 1936, the Bureau of Indian Affairs and the National Park Service agreed on a single residential site south of Furnace Creek Ranch. Approximately 40 acres of land became the Timbisha Shoshone Village.

However, the federal government did not recognize these Death Valley residents officially as a Native American Tribe until 1983; but even then, they were not awarded a permanent land base within their ancestral homeland. Finally, on November 1, 2000, the Timbisha Shoshone Homeland Act became law. It provides for about 300 acres of land near Furnace Creek to be held in trust for the tribe. Additionally, a section of the western part of Death Valley National Park may be designated as the Timbisha Shoshone Natural and Cultural Preservation Area. Within this area, low-impact, environmentally sustainable, tribal traditional uses such as seasonal camping and the gathering of pinyon pine nuts, mesquite beans, and plants for medicinal use, would be allowed. The Timbisha Shoshone now have an active role in management decisions affecting some of their traditional land.

---

**OPPOSITE:** Waterfall in Surprise Canyon, Panamint Mountains. PHOTO© FRED HIRSCHMANN        **PAGE 28/29:** Desert sunflowers and the Furnace Creek badlands. PHOTO© LARRY ULRICH

A glance at a detailed map of the Death Valley area reveals myriad old mines, mill sites, and ghost towns, each with its own story of bright hopes and more likely dashed dreams. Visions of gold, lead, and silver drove many of the prospectors, but it was borax and talc that resulted in the biggest bonanzas. Seven hundred thousand tons of talc were taken out of the Warm Springs Canyon area, and the Boraxo Mine, in upper Furnace Creek Wash, was active until the 1980s. During the latter part of the nineteenth century, borax production was Death Valley's most successful mining venture. The value of Death Valley's talc and borax exceeds all of the heavy metal production combined.

Antimony was discovered in Wildrose Canyon in 1860, but real mining was to emerge slowly. Lead was found in the Cottonwood Mountains and copper around Racetrack Valley, but these mines were limited in scope.

Most of the area's mines started about 1904 and were abandoned by 1930, with the three main ones being gold mines—Bullfrog Hills in the eastern Grapevine Mountains, Skidoo in the Panamints, and the Keane Wonder Mine in the Funeral Range. Unlike the others, these sites had rich ore, and perhaps more importantly, experienced managers who could develop the proper mining and processing infrastructure. Most of the prospectors were hardy individualists, who if they were lucky enough to discover an ore body, usually didn't have the where-with-all to develop it into a paying proposition.

Transporting their ores out of the valley was a major problem. The shortage of water and the oppressive, deadly desert heat added to the arduous task of making money from their claims.

More than once, investors were duped by miners claiming to have found the mother lode, when in reality these were minor, or even nonexistent, deposits. But money flowed, mining companies formed, equipment was purchased, towns were thrown up, followed by dismal results.

Although, the area was established as a national monument in February 1933, Congress re-opened it to prospecting and mining the following June. By the 1950s, most heavy metal mining in the monument was over, but not until the passage of the 1976 Mining in the Parks Act was mining restricted to existing claims.

A few mines are still operating today in the area. The Billie Mine produces borax, and gold mining is being carried out at the south end of the Panamint Valley near Manly Fall.

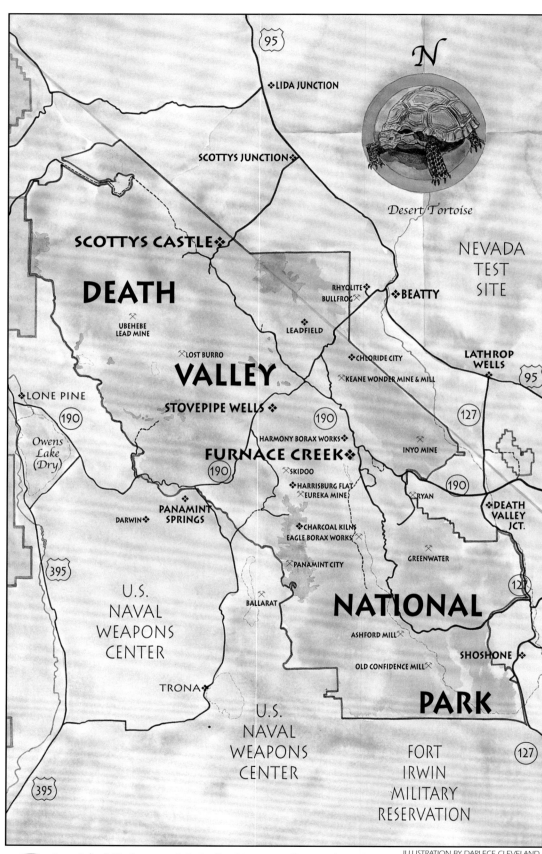

ILLUSTRATION BY DARLECE CLEVELAND

MINES & GHOST TOWNS OF DEATH VALLEY

**OPPOSITE:** Crumbling adobe brick wall at Harmony Borax Works. PHOTO© JEFF GNASS

Ashford Mill.
PHOTO© JEFF D. NICHOLAS

Ore car at Ballarat.
PHOTO© CAROL POLICH

Charcoal Kilns.
PHOTO© PHIL KEMBER

Harrisburg, Cashier Mill.
PHOTO© LAURENCE PARENT

A 27-mile, one-way dirt road runs down dramatic and narrow Titus Canyon, which cuts through the Grapevine Mountains. The range and canyon are geologically recent features, but the limestone that makes up the Grapevines is over half a billion years old, laid down when this part of California was submerged beneath a warm tropical sea. Thousands of feet of limey goo were deposited on the ocean floor, some of it originating from thick mats of calcareous algae (stromatolites).

To access the canyon, leave the park heading east through Daylight Pass toward Beatty, Nevada. Just after passing the "Welcome to Nevada" sign, Titus Canyon Road turns off to the left (north). About a mile down this road, a faint track running off to the southwest marks where Old Dinah, the steam tractor now on display at Furnace Creek Ranch, hauled supplies from the now ghost town of Rhyolite to the Keane Wonder Mine. After crossing the Amargosa Valley, the road crests the Grapevine Mountains at Red Pass and begins its descent into Death Valley.

About three miles beyond Red Pass, is the site of **Leadfield**, which blossomed in 1926 and busted the same year. Promoters claimed a rich deposit of lead, but the real money was in selling mining stock and the 1,749 town lots. Today, the area is scattered with mines, dumps, tunnels, and prospect holes, as well as, the remains of wood and tin buildings, a dugout, and the concrete foundations of the mill.

In another three miles is Klare Springs, a good place to spot desert bighorn sheep and look for Native American petroglyphs. Please do not touch the rock art since skin oils deteriorate the rock. The road now enters a spectacular four-mile narrow section of Titus Canyon (only 20 feet wide in places) before exiting on a broad alluvial fan. You can also drive up to the canyon entrance, park, and hike into the narrows.

**Rhyolite**, the Queen City of Death Valley, is just outside the eastern boundary of the park, but its history is intricately tied to Death Valley. One fine August day in 1904, Shorty Harris and Ed Cross found green-stained quartz scattered all over a hill, "…just full of free gold…it was the original bullfrog rock." The Bullfrog Mining District was established and the rush was on. A townsite was laid out and given the name Rhyolite, the silica-rich volcanic rock found in the area.

During its heyday from 1905-1910, Rhyolite was the area's largest town, boasting a population of up to ten thousand people. There were approximately two churches, 50 saloons, 18 stores, two undertakers, 19 lodging houses, eight doctors, two dentists, a school, an ice plant, three hospitals, a stock exchange, and an opera. The Alaska Glacier Ice Cream Parlor was popular, as well as, the red light district, which drew employees from as far away as San Francisco. Today the town contains numerous ruins, including the famous Bottle House, built from more than 30,000 beer and liquor bottles; the Las Vegas Tonopah Railroad Station; the remains of the three-story Cook Bank building; and the jail. The townsite is on a mixture of private and BLM land, about 35 miles east of the Furnace Creek Visitor Center and four miles west of Beatty.

Two men from Ballarat, Jack Keane and Domingo Etcharren, were prospecting for silver in late 1903 when they discovered quite by accident an immense ledge of free milling gold (i.e. gold that is uncombined with other substances). This became the **Keane Wonder Mine**. By the next spring, a full-blown gold rush to the site was on. A great deal of money was spent developing the mine, but financial problems continually plagued the operation. Despite the problems, the mine eventually produced an estimated $1,100,000 worth of gold by the time it closed in 1942. The Keane Wonder was one of the largest producing gold mines in the Death Valley area.

The **Lost Burro Mine** is located about three miles southeast of Teakettle Junction off Hidden Valley Road. This picturesque site still contains a cabin, an outhouse, and the ruins of the gold mill. In 1907, Bert Shively was rounding up his burros when he noticed a promising deposit. Through the years various owners worked the area and by the time the mine closed in the 1970s, about $100,000 worth of gold had been retrieved.

**Skidoo** was founded in 1906 when two prospectors, on their way to the strike at Harrisburg, discovered gold in Emigrant Canyon. The deposit eventually yielded almost one and a half million dollars worth of gold, making it one of the few truly profitable gold mines in Death Valley. The town grew to 700 souls and became infamous as the only site of a hanging in Death Valley. Hootch Simpson, a saloon owner who had fallen on hard times, tried to rob the bank, was foiled in the attempt, and later went back and killed the owner of the store in which the bank was located. During the night, townspeople lynched Hootch. According to legend, he was hanged twice. The second time was to accommodate news photographers who had missed the fatal first hanging. Skidoo's gold vein played out in 1917. Although it was one of the sites for the 1923 movie "*Greed*", today nothing remains of the town; only an interpretive sign marks the site.

In 1905, Shorty Harris and his Basque partner Jean Pierre "Pete" Aguereberry discovered a gold deposit. The town of **Harrisburg** sprung up but faded within a year. Although most left, Pete kept working his Eureka Mine until he died in 1945. Nothing remains of the town, except Pete's home and mine, which are located on the right about two miles down the road to Aguereberry Point.

In the pinyon pine–juniper woodland of upper Wildrose Canyon, ten 25-foot high, rock-and-mortar **charcoal kilns** were built to supply charcoal for two silver-lead smelters serving investor George Hearst's mines in the Argus Range on the west side on Panamint Valley. Neither coal nor enough trees occurred near the smelters. By 1877, the kilns were completed. Forty-two cords of pinyon wood would be carefully stacked into each kiln; and after a week of smoldering, about 2,000 bushels of charcoal were ready. However by the summer of 1878, the Argus mines were abandoned along with the kilns.

**Ballarat**, founded in 1897, is located off the Panamint Valley road west of Death Valley just outside the park. Ballarat's main mine was the Radcliffe, which produced 15,000 tons of gold ore over a five-year period. The ruins of the town are privately owned (check at the Ballarat store about sightseeing). A dozen miles northeast of Ballarat is the ghost town of Panamint City. Panamint City was called "the toughest, rawest, most hard-boiled little hellhole that ever passed for a town." It was founded by outlaws who, while hiding from the law, stumbled across silver in Surprise Canyon. By 1874, at the height of its boom, the city boasted 2,000 citizens. The next year the boom was over, people left, and a flashflood the following year destroyed most of the town. The chimney of the smelter is the most prominent remnant of the town's heyday. A five-mile hike is necessary to reach this site.

In 1905, word leaked out that a whole mountain of copper had been discovered on the brink of Death Valley. Thousands of hopeful prospectors rushed to the spot. A quarter of a billion dollars in stock was offered to the public. The town of **Greenwater** sprung up, even though water had to be hauled in and sold for $15 a barrel. But after four years, only a couple of thousand dollars-worth of copper had been extracted. Folks grumbled that it was "the monumental mining-stock swindle of the century." Today, there are no ruins marking the site, which is located south of Dantes View on the Greenwater Valley gravel road.

Keane Wonder Mill. PHOTO© JEFF GNASS

Lost Burro Mine. PHOTO© LARRY ULRICH

Cook Bank Building, Rhyolite. PHOTO© CAROL POLICH

Skidoo. PHOTO© TOM TILL

Twenty Mule Team, circa 1930s.

# BORAX AND 20 MULE TEAMS

The real gold of Death Valley was not the hidden metallic kind but the readily exposed white, crystalline mineral composed of sodium, oxygen, boron, and water molecules. Over the last three million years, water percolating through uplifted ancient lakebeds has dissolved soluble borate minerals and carried them to the playa below Furnace Creek Wash. As the mineral-rich water evaporated, various borate minerals, including borax, precipitated out. (More than 25 types of borate minerals occur in Death Valley.) Borax has been valuable for centuries. Marco Polo supposedly brought borax back from Mongolia in the thirteenth century, where the Chinese had been using it in their porcelain glazes. Today, borax is used to remove impurities from molten materials and as a flux in welding. It is also an excellent cleansing agent, antiseptic, and is needed in the manufacture of many types of glass, pharmaceuticals, enamel, fire retardants, gasoline additives, insecticides, and fertilizer. More recently, it has been used in nuclear reactor shields and in the production of fiberglass.

Borax was first noticed in Death Valley in 1873 and "rediscovered" by Rosie and Aaron Winters a couple of miles north of Furnace Creek in 1881. The Winters sold their claim to William Tell Coleman, a controversial San Francisco commission broker and vigilante, for $20,000. Coleman had his Greenland Salt and Borax Company (later called the Harmony Borax Works) erect several adobe and stone buildings, wooden warehouses, a boiler, and 36 huge crystallization tanks. Production began in late 1883.

Nodules of borate, called "cottonballs", were gathered by Chinese laborers off of Cottonball Marsh and carted to Harmony, where the borates were dissolved in boiling water. The solution was then drained into settling tanks to allow the borax to precipitate onto iron rods. The process worked well except during the hottest part of the summer when the solution would not cool enough to allow the borax to crystallize.

Between 1883 and 1888, the borax was hauled out of the valley using the legendary twenty-mule teams, which were usually nine teams of mules and a pair of draft horses at the rear. Each team pulled two enormous wagons each loaded with ten tons of borax and a 1,200-gallon water tank—a total hauling weight of 36 tons. Driving such an unwieldy rig took an especially adept muleskinner. The trip from Harmony to the nearest railhead was a rough 165 miles to Mojave and took ten or more days one-way. The romance and adventure associated with these twenty-mule teams from Death Valley became an advertising symbol for the U.S. Borax Company and for the popular radio and later television show "*Death Valley Days*," which it sponsored.

But after just five years of operation, the Harmony Borax Works shut down when deposits of a mineral containing higher concentrations of boron (later named colemanite) were discovered much closer to the railheads and a financially over-extended Coleman went bankrupt.

The Harmony Borax Ruins and the crumbling townsite can be easily visited. A walk into Cottonball Basin is a haunting experience. At the Furnace Creek Ranch complex is the Borax Museum, which has displays that chronicle the history of Death Valley.

**OPPOSITE:** Harmony Borax Works and Telescope Peak. PHOTO© LARRY ULRICH       **PAGE 36/37:** Charcoal kilns and distant Sierra Nevada. PHOTO© LAURENCE PARENT

Ornately tiled kitchen of Scottys Castle.

# SCOTTY AND HIS CASTLE

Listen carefully up in Grapevine Canyon on a quiet fall day. Are those the sweet strains of Bach played on a pipe organ? Or is it water splashing in a fountain? Or just ghostly whispers on the desert wind?

Death Valley Scotty is one of the area's most enduring characters. Born Walter Scott in 1872, he ran away from his Kentucky home to join his brother on a ranch in Nevada. In 1890, Buffalo Bill Cody's Wild West Show hired Scott. After traveling the world with the show for 12 years, he began a new profession—gold prospecting. He convinced several wealthy businessmen that he had found a gold deposit in Death Valley worth a fortune. All he needed was some seed money to develop the mine. Gold from the mine was not forthcoming, but Scott was often seen in the finest hotels and saloons of California and Nevada, spending his investors' money freely.

One of his most loyal investors was Chicago insurance magnate Albert Johnson. After investing thousands of dollars, Johnson decided he wanted to see Scotty's gold mine for himself in 1906. Scotty took Johnson on a grueling horseback trip through Death Valley, hoping that the investor would become discouraged and return home. Instead, Johnson fell in love with the valley and seemed to thrive in the dry, sunny climate. Although he never saw Scotty's alleged mine, Johnson did not seem to mind. He liked the eccentric desert rat.

Over the next decade, Johnson and his wife Bessie Penniman often returned to Death Valley to explore the desert with Scotty. Bessie, who referred to herself as "a little desert mouse traveling with two big desert rats," suggested that since she and her husband were spending so much time there that a comfortable house instead of a tent would be in order.

Recognizing a good story, Scotty told everyone that he was building the two million dollar, 25-room Moorish-style mansion and nine surrounding outbuildings in Grapevine Canyon from his gold mine profits. When questioned, Johnson would agree with Scotty and pass himself off as Scotty's banker.

The 1929 Stock Market Crash and ensuing Great Depression had its impact even in remote Death Valley. By 1931, most of the workmen were gone and further construction to Death Valley Ranch, more popularly known as Scotty's Castle, came to a halt. The ranch was never completed. Toward the end of the Great Depression, the Johnsons retired to Hollywood and often visited the ranch, which became a popular hotel and tourist attraction. Thousands of tourists came each year to what they thought was the home of one of the world's richest gold miners. Scotty actually spent most of his time in a simple, private cabin a few miles west of there.

The Johnsons died in the 1940s, and having no heirs, willed the ranch to their Gospel Foundation of California, which continued to run the hotel business and tours. The foundation cared for Scotty, who lived at the "castle" the last two years of his life. He died in 1954 at the age of 82 and was laid to rest on a hill overlooking the ranch. In 1970, the National Park Service acquired the property, and rangers, in period clothing, present 1939-style living history tours daily.

**OPPOSITE:** Scottys Castle. PHOTO© TERRY DONNELLY

# THE LANDSCAPE

Virga rain over the Grapevine Mountains.  PHOTO© RANDI HIRSCHMANN

 We entered the park from the south on a badly washboarded road, crossed the several, shallow ribbons of gray Amargosa River and continued to Saratoga Springs. The skies were lead and even a couple of raindrops fell as we emerged from the car. A lot of nothingness and the fact that it was spring didn't stop the cold wind blowing down off the Panamints.

Coots, American widgeons, and a mallard cruised on one of the ponds. Several salt encrusted bunny turds sat inside a coyote track pressed into the soft mud at the pond's edge. The reeds and bulrushes crowding the brackish pool rubbed together making a desert song similar to faint red-winged blackbird calls. The pond's water was stained iron brown; sulfurous odors wafted on the wind. Saltbush, saltgrass, iodinebush, and other halophytes flourished in the salty soil. A Say's phoebe took wing but a gust blew the bird away. Smaller, faster swallows darted over the water somehow catching a meal of flying insects.

The clouds dissolved as we headed north. We grabbed a latte at the petite French café in Shoshone (or was that a mirage?). From town, Highway 178 eased over Salsberry Pass and Jubilee Pass then dropped and dropped AND DROPPED into the Badwater Basin. We took a break at a large alluvial fan emerging from a canyon and strolled across the gentle sloping surface. Fluttering around us was a blizzard of orange and black wings. Hundreds of delicate painted lady butterflies moved like a squall across the harsh land. Individuals would drop and stop briefly on a desert gold, globemallow, or other wildflower blossom, taste with their feet (as all butterflies do), and suck up a drink of nectar with their long proboscis, then launch themselves back into the clear desert air.

This particular spring had been unusually wet bringing forth myriad desert flowers. Notch-leaf phacelia, golden evening primrose, gravel ghost, desert trumpet, and pebble pincushion, if not spectacular in density, were at least remarkable in their variety. We sprawled on the ground to see diminutive Bigelow monkeyflower and other "belly flowers" up close.

Between the flowers, harvester ants busied themselves carrying bits of vegetation back to their subterranean home. A southern desert horned lizard darted to the line of ants and licked several up. Mistakenly called horny toads, horned lizards are true lizards not amphibians. I would never have noticed the lizard if it hadn't moved; it's body coloration matched the ground almost perfectly.

Tucked under a sheltering ledge was a packrat nest. I remembered that several of the '49ers had sampled what they thought was some kind of wilderness peanut brittle deposited in the cliffs. "We found it sweet but sickish…(those who had) a good meal of it were a little troubled with nausea afterwards." What they had eaten was amberat, the accumulation of countless years worth of packrat droppings and urine. A century later, scientists would discover that amberat may be more than 50,000 years old and contains plant parts and pollen from long-gone past environments. I didn't feel like having a snack.

At the base of the nest rested a tiny scorpion, a creature that has changed little in the 350 to 400 million years since it climbed from the sea and became one of the first terrestrial arthropods. Fortunately, there are no scorpions in Death Valley considered deadly to humans. During the hippie days of the late 1960s, someone playing with a blacklight in the desert noticed that scorpions fluoresce under ultraviolet light. Taking a blacklight out on a warm moonless night will reveal just how frighteningly common scorpions are.

On the road again, we passed Furnace Creek Ranch. Just beyond the visitor center a coyote, head held low, lurked behind some tamarisk. He had no doubt been spoiled from handouts from tourists. Not only can human food sicken wildlife but their association of food with visitors puts both animal and visitor at risk.

We continued on Highway 190 past Stovepipe Wells where we began the long ascent toward Towne Pass, then turned left on to Emigrant Canyon Road. As we climbed to over 5,000 feet elevation, the rolling terrain covered by scrubby blackbrush backed by distant snowy peaks reminded me a little of the Peruvian Altiplano. We left the Mojave Desert behind and entered more typical Great Basin Desert—an arid habitat where plants and animals struggle to cope

**OPPOSITE:** Desert sunflowers near the mouth of Golden Canyon. PHOTO© LARRY ULRICH

Racetrack Playa and edge of The Grandstand.

not only with extremely hot summer temperatures but bitter winter cold, too.

We turned up Wildrose Canyon and were stopped by snow-drifts near the abandoned charcoal kilns. But we came prepared. Out come cross-country skis, and off we went for a little tour through the pinyon and juniper woodland. The snow was break-able crust so the skiing sucked but the scenery was glorious. A flock of pinyon jays made a ruckus as they winged past. No doubt they were complaining about the snow, too. After it melted, though, they would be able to retrieve the thousands of pine nuts they had cached in the ground the previous summer and fall. Those seeds forgotten, of course, germinate into new woodlands. In the fading light, we gave up trying to make nice sinuous turns back to the car and simply crouched down on our skis and used them like tobog-gans.

Death Valley, although harsh, dangerous, unforgiving, is definitely not a dead place. It is a delicate, fragile window to the natural world's intricacies. Here the mosaic of living communities performs the day-to-day, the millennia-to-millennia dance of evolution. Some partners sit out and disappear while others swing and improvise to the genetic flow. The flora and fauna are not scattered at random across the landscape but are distributed in an orderly fashion into distinct communities or as pioneering ecolo-gist Clinton Hart Merriam phrased it—life zones. And though Merriam's life zone idea is an oversimplification, that doesn't lessen the fact that nature is extraordinarily ordered, complex, and unendingly marvelous, even in Death Valley.

The dunes of Mesquite Flat.

PHOTO© CAROL POLICH

# The Dunes of Death Valley

A popular image of the desert is one of endless sand dunes. In fact, sand dunes are a rather uncommon feature of North American deserts, including the Death Valley area. However, there are several beautiful dune fields within the park. The most accessible are the Mesquite Flat Dunes, just northeast of Stovepipe Wells. Other dune fields are located in the Panamint Valley, Saline Valley, near the Ibex Hills, and in remote Eureka Valley.

Dunes are dynamic. They change shape, texture, size, even orientation after each major windstorm. The sand originates from the weathering of bedrock into grains of quartz or feldspar. The wind transports the sand in three different ways—grains can be pushed along or bounced, which frosts the surface of the grain, or nudged along by impact from bouncing or blowing grains. When the wind stops or forms an eddy, the sand settles. The sand piles into dunes whose shapes are determined by the direction and force of the prevailing zephyrs.

On a particular dune, the wind continues to move sand to the top of the pile until the pile is so steep that it collapses under its own weight. The collapsing sand comes to rest, its angle of repose, when it reaches just the right steepness, around 30-34°, to keep the dune stable. This repeating cycle of sand inching up the windward side to the dune crest, then slipping down the steeper slip face allows the dune to slowly migrate over time. If vegetation becomes established on the dunes, it may eventually stabilize them and prevent further movement. If the dunes become buried by later sediments and through the eons cemented into sandstone, the sloping laminations may become fossilized and later revealed as crossbedding.

The Mesquite Flat Dunes are an assemblage of mostly short transverse dune ridges. For some unknown reason, four ridges have converged at a single point to form a star dune in the northeast corner of the field.

Dunes in the Eureka field tower more than 650 feet above the valley floor, among the highest in California. This dune field receives more precipitation than the other park dunes, thus has a greater diversity and abundance of flora and fauna. Sand may seem unlikely as an oasis, but rain soaks in and then is insulated from rapid evaporation. More than 50 species of plants grow on this dune field, three of them endemics—Eureka Dunes evening primrose (*Oenothera californica eurekensis*), Eureka Valley dune grass (*Swallenia alexandrae*), and shining milkvetch (*Astragalus lentiginosus micans*). Unfortunately, invasive exotic weeds, such as tumbleweed, compete with the natives.

Take a short walk into the dunes and admire the animal tracks. Look for the tractor tread of a stink beetle, the curious J-shaped tracks of a passing sidewinder, or the "pogo" depressions of a fleeing fringe-toed lizard. If it is very quiet and you are very lucky, you may hear a throbbing sound similar to a bass violin or the lower notes of a pipe organ. The Eureka Dunes are one of the rare types known as "singing dunes." The moisture content, grain size, and surface texture all play roles in producing the mystifying sandy song.

**PAGE 44/45:** Early morning light on Mesquite Flat Dunes and the Grapevine Mountains. PHOTO© CARR CLIFTON

# DEATH VALLEY NATIONAL PARK

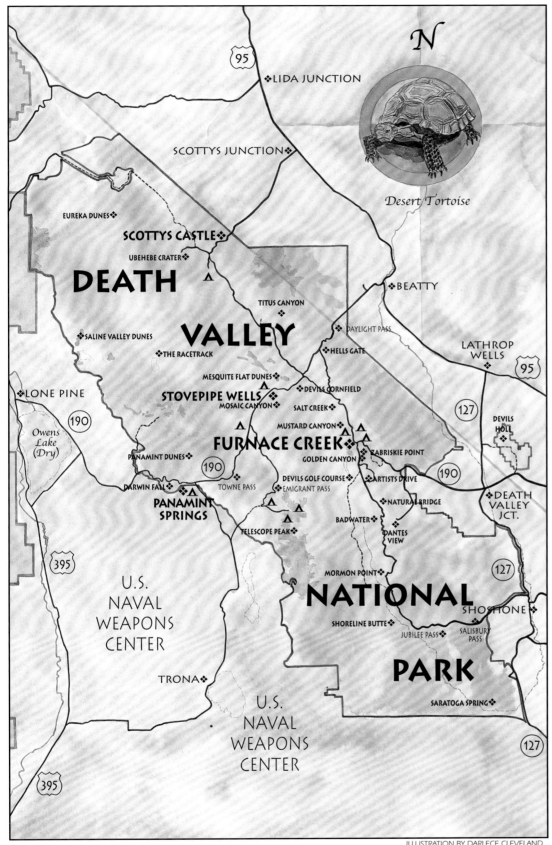

Desert Tortoise

ILLUSTRATION BY DARLECE CLEVELAND

President Franklin D. Roosevelt established the Civilian Conservation Corps in 1933 as one means to put people back to work and help pull the country out of the Great Depression. Starting in October of that year, members of the CCC came to the fledgling national monument and spent the next nine years building barracks, grading 500 miles of roads, installing water and telephone lines, building trails to scenic points, and erecting buildings for themselves and the National Park Service. They constructed five campgrounds, restroom and picnic facilities, developed springs and wells, and built an airplane landing strip. They also helped in building an adobe village, laundry, and trading post for the Timbisha Shoshone. Without their hard work, early tourists would have had a much more difficult time visiting Death Valley. The eruption of World War Two ended the CCC program.

Remember: this park is big, twice the size of Delaware. The distances you need to travel between sights and facilities are great. Keep this in mind when planning your trip.

The park is open year-round, and the first-time visitor should definitely make a stop at Furnace Creek Visitor Center and Death Valley Museum to learn about the park's human and natural history and about safe travel through the desert. This visitor center also has an excellent selection of books and other materials dealing with Death Valley and the region. A short orientation film is shown at frequent intervals in the center's auditorium.

Other museums or information centers are found at Scotty's Castle, the Eastern Sierra Interagency Visitor Center a few miles south of Lone Pine, and the Borax Museum at Furnace Creek Ranch. Ranger stations are located at Stovepipe Wells, Grapevine, and in Shoshone and Beatty.

Accommodations in the park are limited to Panamint Springs Resort, Stovepipe Wells Village, Furnace Creek Ranch, and Furnace Creek Inn. Outside the park, lodging can be found in Beatty, Amargosa Valley, Stateline, Death Valley Junction, Shoshone, and Lone Pine. Some are open only seasonally and fill early, so call ahead for a reservation.

Today's stores and gas stations at Scotty's Castle, Stovepipe Wells Village, and Furnace Creek Ranch are a far cry from Burro Bill and Edna's rustic 1930s Trading Post on Salt Creek. Radiator water is available at a number of locations throughout the park. Refer to the free park service visitor map and newspaper, or their web site, for current information.

## NATURAL FEATURES OF DEATH VALLEY

**OPPOSITE:** Salt pinnacles of Devils Golf Course and the Panamint Mountains. PHOTO© PHIL KEMBER

Artists Palette. PHOTO© BRUCE JACKSON/GNASS PHOTO IMAGES

Devils Golf Course. PHOTO© ROBERT HILDEBRAND

Mosaic Canyon. PHOTO© JEFF D. NICHOLAS

Natural Bridge. PHOTO© HERBERT SCHOLZ

**Ubehebe Crater**, in the northern part of the park, is an eerie, surreal place. Three thousand years ago (new findings suggest an age of only 300 years) an upward-migrating mass of basaltic magma, following the fault near the base of Tin Mountain, encountered water-soaked bedrock and alluvial fan sediments. Practically instantaneously, the water flashed into steam resulting in a deafening explosion, propelling rocky debris along the ground at up to 100 miles/hour, and blowing a 770-foot deep hole in the ground called a maar crater. Over a dozen other explosion craters and tuff rings found in the Ubehebe area are also the result of this type of hydrovolcanic eruption.

Immediately west of Stovepipe Wells Village, a gravel road climbs an alluvial fan toward Tucki Mountain. The mouth of **Mosaic Canyon** is reached in about 2.4 miles. A short, quarter-mile walk leads into Mosaic Canyon's twisting narrows, made of smooth polished marble. The marble was formed from Late Precambrian dolomite and other carbonate rocks when these rocks were buried under younger sediments. Unfathomable pressure over time folded and metamorphosed the relatively soft carbonates into hard marble.

On the canyon floor, just south of the parking area, notice the "mosaic" of marble and fragments of other rock cemented together. Geologists call formations composed of angular fragments breccia.

A must-stop is **Zabriskie Point** named after Christian Breevort Zabriskie, one-time vice president and general manager of Pacific Coast Borax and tourist promoter. From here, you look out across a scene of terrible desolation. Mustard yellow and coffee brown mudstones have been intricately carved into barren badlands that in the morning or late afternoon light become an artist's or photographer's dreamscape. To your right, the particularly impressive shark's tooth-shaped hill is called Manly Beacon, although it is

doubtful that 1849 argonaut William Lewis Manly noticed it.

**Artist's Drive** takes the visitor along the face of the Black Mountains. The curvy, one-way, one-lane drive cuts through the multicolored Artist Drive Formation. This palette of pink, green, purple, brown, and black volcanic ash and basaltic rock is the result of one of Death Valley's most violently explosive volcanic periods, some eight to six million years ago.

A paved road once meandered through **Golden Canyon**. But in February 1976, a four-day storm dropped more than two inches of rain at Furnace Creek. On the morning of the fourth day, a violent downpour sent a tremendous surge of water, rock, and mud down the canyon and swept away the road.

Today, this is one of the easiest and most beautiful hikes in the park (but still dangerous if rain is threatening). The narrow canyon is cut through an ancient alluvial fan. The poorly sorted conglomerate was laid down some five to six million years ago, subsequently buried, and then cemented into solid rock known as the Furnace Creek Formation. Recent uplift and erosion have exposed it.

Continuing up the canyon, the conglomerate gives way to fine-grained, relatively soft, light-yellow mudstones that were deposited on the bottom of a lake. Occasionally ripple marks were preserved. Within the mudstone are white bands of evaporite minerals such as halite (table salt), gypsum, and borax. These layers formed in the same manner as those evaporite deposits seen on the floor of Death Valley. The lack of plants is primarily due to the clay in these badlands. When the clay gets wet, it swells thereby preventing moisture from soaking in and depriving plants of water.

Near the head of the Golden Canyon is the 400-foot-high wall known as the **Red Cathedral**. It is made of iron oxide-stained fanglomerate, whose origin was from another ancient alluvial fan.

Natural bridges and arches are not common in Death Valley National Park, but there are several worth visiting. The easiest to visit is **Natural Bridge** in the north-central part of the Black Mountains. A short one-third-mile trail leads to this massive geologic feature. A geology exhibit at the trailhead helps explain its origin. Other notable natural stone spans include **Little Bridge**, in a canyon of the same name on the eastern slope of Tucki Mountain, and **Eye of the Needle**, an arch in Echo Canyon.

In 1860, a group of silver prospectors looking for the Lost Gunsight Lode entered the west side of the Panamint Range. One of them climbed the highest peak and proclaimed that he had only seen farther using a telescope. Today, 11,049-foot-high **Telescope Peak**, the highest point in the park, is a strenuous but rewarding hike. The 14-mile round-trip trail, constructed by the Civilian Conservation Corps in the mid-1930s, begins on the south side of the Mahogany Flat parking area (8,133 feet). After several miles, the trail passes through Arcane Meadow and enters a scattered stand of gnarled bristlecone pine, some of which may be more than 3,000 years old. John Thorndyke, an early miner, dreamed of building a hotel on the peak but ended up with several tourist cabins located at what is now Thorndike Campground.

A 1934 park service guidebook described the saltpan at the north end of the 200-square-mile Badwater Basin as a place where "only the devil could play golf on such a surface." The **Devils Golf Course** is a remnant of the shallow lake that evaporated about 2,000 years ago. As the lake dried, calcite and other carbonates precipitated first. Sulfates such as gypsum came next and finally chlorides, especially sodium chloride, ordinary table salt. The exposed precipitates are three to five feet thick, and overlie 9,000 feet of older sediments and salts.

The intricate salt pinnacles form when salty water rises up from underlying muds. Capillary action draws the saline water upward where it quickly evaporates, leaving salt crystals behind. The pinnacles grow very slowly, perhaps as little as an inch in 35 years. Wind and rain erode them into fantastic shapes. On a still, summer morning, you may hear tiny pops and pings as salt crystals expand and burst in the growing heat of the day. Imagine the 1849 pioneers trying to cross this rough terrain.

The **West Side Road** roughly follows the 1850 route of the Bennett and Arcan families past Bennett's Well, where they waited 26 days for help. (Some historians believe the actual site might be at Eagle Borax Spring or three miles farther north at Tule Spring.) The road passes the Eagle Borax Works, the first borax operation in Death Valley, and the graves of prospectors Jim Dayton and Shorty Harris. The road also provides access to the four main canyons cut into the eastern flank of the Panamint Range—Trail, Hanaupah, Johnson, and Warm Springs.

In the extreme southeast corner of the park is **Saratoga Springs**, three large ponds that were once a stop on the twenty-mule team route between the Amargosa Borax Works (not far from Tecopa Hot Springs) and Daggett. A group of geologists encamped here in 1900 put up a sign: "20 miles from wood, 20 miles from water, 40 feet from Hell, God bless our home!" This rare desert alkali marsh wetland supports common reed, bulrush, and saltgrass. The endemic Saratoga Springs pupfish lives only here, as well as, five very rare invertebrates—the Amargosa tryonia snail, the Amargosa spring snail, the Saratoga Springs belostoma bug, the Amargosa naucorid bug, and the Death Valley June beetle. Besides these endemic species there is a host of birds that utilize the springs, notably the yellow warbler, Cooper's hawk, western snowy plover, long-billed curlew, and long-eared owl. The springs are also one of the few locations in the park where red-spotted toads and Pacific treefrogs occur together.

Saratoga Spring. PHOTO© FRED HIRSCHMANN

Ubehebe Crater. PHOTO© JEFF D. NICHOLAS

West Side Drive near Shorty's Well. PHOTO© ERIC WUNROW

Dramatic dawn at Zabriskie Point. PHOTO© LARRY CARVER

Zig-zag tracks created by "moving" rocks, the Racetrack.

# THE RACETRACK

At the end of a rough, 28-mile dirt road, in a park blessed with many strange and mysterious features, one of the oddest has to be the Racetrack. In a remote closed-in valley located south-southwest of Ubehebe Crater, there is a *playa*, or dry lakebed, that is home to wandering rocks. Here rocks up to 700 pounds move mysteriously when no one is looking. The stones leave a trail behind them and occasionally push mud into tiny rills in front. Some tracks are arrow-straight, but others meander. Some tracks are quite short while others are nearly 3,000 feet long.

Playas are some of the flattest and smoothest landforms on earth. During periods of heavy rain, water collects on the playa to form a shallow lake. As the water evaporates, a soft layer of mud is left. As the mud dries, it shrinks and cracks into an intricate mosaic of interlocking polygons. The south end of Racetrack Playa abuts a steep, 850-foot mountain face composed of dolomite, a calcium-magnesium carbonate. Stones falling from this face supply the playa with most of its moving rocks.

What force is responsible for this outlandish lithic behavior? The shallow furrows and rounded, levee-like ridges that form the trails imply the stones move only when the playa surface is soft and wet. To solve the mystery, scientists monitored more than 160 rocks (and gave each one a woman's name) and their trails using Global Positioning System instruments. The longest, straightest trails are concentrated in the southeastern part of the playa. In this area, wind is channeled through a low point in the mountains forming a natural wind tunnel. In the central part of the playa, two natural wind tunnels focus their energy from different directions, and it's here that the trails are the most convoluted. Surprisingly, trail lengths and headings are not well correlated with rock shape, volume, or area of surface contact.

The evidence suggests that strong gusts of wind and swirling dust devils, in combination with a slick mud surface, set rocks in motion. At least that's the conclusion until someone actually witnesses the strange event. And some rocks simply defy all reason. Karen, a 700-pound rectangular block, rested on an old, straight 570-foot-long track and didn't budge during the seven-year study. Then one day, she was gone.

---

**OPPOSITE:** Circular track left by "moving" rock, The Racetrack. PHOTO© RANDY PRENTICE          **PAGE 52/53:** Panamint Mountains and flooded salt pan, sunset. PHOTO© TERRY DONNELLY

Badlands bordering Salt Creek, early morning.

# THE PUPFISH OF SALT CREEK

Desert fish? An oxymoron? At the end of the Pleistocene, as Lake Manly evaporated, the great river system feeding the lake became intermittent. The ancestral fishes that thrived in these waters became isolated from each other, and new species evolved.

One of the most isolated pools is Devils Hole, a detached part of the park located in Ash Meadows National Wildlife Refuge in Nevada. From 200 to 700 Devils Hole pupfish (*Cyprinodon diabolis*) live in an area of about 23 square yards within a larger pool, where the water temperature remains between 91° and 93° F. The fish grow to be about an inch long and live about a year. They primarily feed on algae but will take the occasional beetle, amphipod, or snail. Males sport a metallic, bluish iridescence that changes to metallic green or golden in different light. The female is more yellowish.

The Amargosa River pupfish (*Cyprinodon nevadensis amargosa*) and its very close relative, the Saratoga Springs pupfish (*C. n. nevadensis*), are effective predators on mosquito larvae although their main food is algae.

The breeding males are blue with a black band at the end of the tail; females have additional vertical bands. Their maximum size is 2.5 inches and they probably live two to three years. Apparently these pupfish can withstand water temperatures ranging from near freezing to 107° Fahrenheit.

Remarkably, the Salt Creek pupfish (*Cyprinodon salinus*) and Cottonball Marsh pupfish (*Cyprinodon milleri*) are able to survive in one of the harshest environments in Death Valley. The former are confined to a 1.5-mile stretch of Salt Creek, which originates on Mesquite Flat, and the latter to Cottonball Marsh near the Salt Creek Sink, where the water can be nearly five times saltier than the ocean. Breeding males are deep blue with an iridescent purple back. They grow to 1.5 inches and probably live less than a year. Their diet is probably similar to the other pupfish. Their population fluctuates wildly with changes in water flows. When water is abundant, Salt Creek pupfish may number in the millions, but as the creek shrinks and water temperatures go up, fish die by the thousands. Ravens, killdeer, and great blue herons dine on the little fish. During the winter, the pupfish may hibernate in the mud on the creek bottom. Salt Creek's boardwalk trail is an excellent way to get a glimpse of these unique, endemic fish.

**OPPOSITE:** Badlands of Gower Gulch seen from Zabriskie Point. PHOTO© JEFF GNASS

Mountain lion.  PHOTO© TOM & PAT LEESON

Desert bighorns.  PHOTO© FRANK S. BALTHIS

Coyote.  PHOTO© FRANK S. BALTHIS

Most of Death Valley's mammals avoid the heat of the day by being nocturnal or crepuscular, spending the day deep inside a burrow or in the shade. Some skip summer entirely by aestivating. However, the white-tailed antelope ground squirrel (*Ammospermophilus leucurus*) may be seen scurrying about in the sun with its tail held over its back like a parasol. This ground squirrel can withstand very high body temperatures without injury or death. If the animal does get too hot, it will lick its fur for evaporative cooling or flatten its body against the shaded ground to "unload" heat.

A black-tailed jackrabbit (*Lepus californicus*) may be startled out from under its hiding place during the day. It sits quietly in the shade with its large, well-vasculated ears facing the sky. Those ears act as radiators and help cool the bunny.

There are 51 native species of mammals in Death Valley National Park and at least two exotics—horses and burros. Bats account for about 30 percent of the species, and rodents make up about half of the species. The largest native mammal is the Nelson desert bighorn (*Ovis canadensis nelsoni*); perhaps 500 to 1000 individuals reside in the park, usually not far from water. At less then 3.75 inches long, the smallest mammal is the desert shrew (*Notiosorex crawfordii*), a resident of sagebrush habitats. It obtains most of its water from the soft body parts of their prey, which consists mainly of spiders, centipedes, and a variety of insects.

The southern grasshopper mouse (*Onychomys torridus*) is vociferous and voracious and has been described as "howling like a wolf and attacking like a lion." A bit of an exaggeration, but it does behave quite differently from most mice. Grasshopper mice rear up on their hind legs, use their tail for balance, point their head upwards, and emit a tiny squeak, the so-called howl. They also make ultrasonic calls. Then they're off searching for food, not seeds and vegetation, but invertebrates, reptiles, and even the occasional rodent up to three times their size. Cannibalism is not uncommon. The actions of these aggressive and combative mice have been likened to those of shrews. Thus the phrase "Be a man or be a mouse" takes on new meaning.

The park is home to four species of kangaroo rats (*Dipodomys* spp.) and four of pocket mice (*Perognathus* spp.). These rodents can survive without drinking free water. As their bodies metabolize the carbos and fats in dry seeds, water is created. These mammals have no sweat glands, a complex nasal passageway that recovers water vapor as the animal exhales, extremely efficient kidneys that produce urine twice as concentrated as sea water, feces five times drier than a lab rat's droppings, and only come out of their burrows at night—which in concert conserves the metabolic water.

Bobcat.  PHOTO© FRANK S. BALTHIS

Kit fox.  PHOTO© FRANK S. BALTHIS

Kangaroo rat.  PHOTO© GLENN VAN NIMWEGEN

Side-blotched lizard.　　PHOTO© CAROL POLICH

Sidewinder rattlesnake.　　PHOTO© CAROL POLICH

Chuckwalla.　　PHOTO© FRANK S. BALTHIS

Lizards and snakes are usually associated with deserts, and the park has a good representation, 38 reptiles (one tortoise, 18 lizards, and 19 snakes) in all. Surprisingly this desert country also has three native and two introduced species of amphibians.

The two most commonly seen lizards are the zebra-tailed (*Callisaurus draconoides*) and side-blotched (*Uta stansburiana*). The zebra-tailed lizard runs at great speed, with its banded tail curled forward. The small, rather non-descript side-blotched is one of the most abundant lizards in the arid West. It feeds on insects, scorpions, spiders, mites, and ticks.

Lumbering along like a boulder with legs, the endangered desert tortoise (*Gopherus agassizi*) is a curious desert denizen. It is found between 1,000 and 4,000 feet in elevation on sandy or gravel desert, typically where creosote occurs. The tortoise emerges from its burrow in late winter to feed and mate and remains active through spring. Some emerge

again after the summer rains. It eats a wide variety of grasses and the flowers of annuals. Like some humans, it reaches maturity between age 14 and 20 and can live up to 80 years. Unfortunately, about 98 percent of the young tortoises die before reaching maturity. Wonderfully adapted to desert living, they can survive more than a year without access to free water.

Two very rare lizard species are known to occur in the park—the Panamint alligator lizard (*Elgaria panamintina*) and Mojave fringe-toed lizard (*Uma scoparia*). The fringe-toed lizards are especially adapted to living in sandy habitats. Earflaps, large eyelid fringes, and valves that close the nostrils help keep sand out of those orifices. Scale fringes on the bottom of their toes act like snowshoes in helping the lizard navigate across soft sand, where they can attain speeds of more than 10 miles per hour. The desert banded gecko (*Coleonyx variegatus variegatus*)

is one of the few lizards active at night and also has a voice. These pale, soft, delicate creatures spend the day hiding under a rock.

The heavy-bodied chuckwalla (*Sauromalus obesus*) may be seen feeding on flowers and other vegetation but more often are heard when they wedge themselves in a crevice. They inflate their bodies, which causes their scales to rub on the rock surfaces and make an audible noise. Chuckwallas were a favorite food of Native Americans.

Snakes are not common in Death Valley. In sandy areas, look for a series of unconnected, parallel, J-like markings—the tracks of the Mojave Desert sidewinder (*Crotalus cerastes cerastes*). The Panamint rattlesnake (*Crotalus mitchelli stephensi*) occurs mainly in higher rocky places up to 7,000 feet. More commonly seen are the coachwhip (*Masticophus flagellum piceus*) and Great Basin gopher snake (*Pituophis melanoleucus deserticola*).

Great Basin gopher snake.　　PHOTO© FRANK S. BALTHIS

Desert horned lizard.　　PHOTO© GENE & JASON STONE/ LEESON PHOTOGRAPHY

Desert tortoise.　　PHOTO© GENE & JASON STONE/ LEESON PHOTOGRAPHY

Western bluebird.                    PHOTO© TOM & PAT LEESON

Red-tailed hawk.                     PHOTO© FRANK S. BALTHIS

Roadrunner.                          PHOTO© TOM & PAT LEESON

More than 346 species of birds have been recorded in Death Valley National Park; many are migrants or winter visitors, some are accidentals. Only about 15 species are common year-round residents. For a desert, a remarkable number of shorebirds migrate through, utilizing the various freshwater and salt marshes. Non-resident pied-billed grebes, great blue herons, and mallards may be observed year-round.

Furnace Creek Ranch, with its relatively lush vegetation and permanent water, is a magnet for migrants, which may include Bewick's wren, western bluebird, American robin, black-throated gray warbler, water pipit, and northern flicker. The silky black phainopepla, another "snowbird," may be seen perched in the tops of mesquite feeding on mistletoe berries, its favorite food. Also found in mesquites are the handsome gray, black and white loggerhead shrike and mockingbird.

Few birds are ground nesters; most require trees or large shrubs, which in the park are usually restricted to permanent water sources. Some of the riparian-dependent birds include black-headed grosbeak, blue grosbeak, song sparrow, warbling vireo, Wilson's warbler, yellow-breasted chat, and common yellowthroat, plus the federally endangered southwestern willow flycatcher and least Bell's vireo.

A ubiquitous permanent resident is the sagacious common raven. Adaptable is an understatement. Ravens survive all climates—from burning deserts to the frigid arctic. Their glossy black feathers absorb solar radiation, and soft downy underfeathers keep heat away from the body. So even on the hottest days, ravens can be observed soaring on thermals with flat, horizontally held wings. Accompanying them may be a red-tailed hawk.

Yes, roadrunners do exist; but no, they do not cry, "Beep Beep." The greater roadru-

nner is a member of the cuckoo family. One tall tale relates how a roadrunner, upon finding a sleeping rattlesnake, will build a fence of cactus joints around it. However, the facts are no less impressive. The roadrunner can reach running speeds of 15 miles per hour. It can fly, but rarely does. It is a very effective predator, capturing snakes, lizards, large insects, rodents, and small birds. On cool mornings, the bird erects its feathers to expose its darkly pigmented skin to the sun, thus heating its body without unnecessary expenditure of metabolic energy.

The black-throated sparrow is well equipped for desert living since it doesn't have to drink nor get moisture directly from its food. Instead, like kangaroo rats and pocket mice, it metabolizes the carbohydrates and fats in seeds to manufacture water.

Mockingbird.                         PHOTO© FRANK S. BALTHIS

Ravens.                              PHOTO© RANDI HIRSCHMANN

American avocet.                     PHOTO© TOM & PAT LEESON

Panamint daisy.                    PHOTO© FRED HIRSCHMANN

Desert five spot.                    PHOTO© LARRY ULRICH

Brittlebush.                    PHOTO© FRED HIRSCHMANN

More than 1,000 flowering plant species are found within the park. Highly anticipated are wet winters and springs that can produce amazing wildflower displays. The best usually occur after the valley has received at least twice the annual average 1.9 inches. Then ephemerals like desert gold (*Geraea canescens*), sand verbena (*Abronia villosa*), and phacelia (*Phacelia* spp.) "cover" the valley floor and alluvial fans. The most common perennial plant is creosote (*Larrea tridentata*). The northern limit of the creosote also marks the northern limit of the Mojave Desert.

Extremes in temperature and moisture availability along with a great variety of substrates, ranging from alkali soils to sand to rock, have been a catalyst for the evolution of plant species found nowhere else. Some of these endemics include hollyleaf four pod spurge (*Tetracoccus ilicifolius*), napkinring eriogonum (*Eriogonum intrafractum*), Gilman sandpaper-plant (*Petalonyx gilmanii*),

Panamint lupine (*Lupinus magnificus*), Death Valley sage (*Salvia funera*), and the rare rocklady maurandya (*Maurandya petrophila*) and rock mimulus (*Mimulus rupicola*).

The general paucity of cacti may surprise those new to the Mojave Desert, although about 15 species, including cottontop (*Echinocactus polycephalus*), strawtop cholla (*Opuntia echinocarpa*), old man pricklypear (*Opuntia erinacea*) and beavertail (*Opuntia basilaris*), occur in the park. The cold temperatures of the mountains limit cactus growth at higher elevations, and the valley floor's salinity prevents them from growing there.

Riparian and spring habitats are like biological islands in the desert sea. Near fresh water can often be found Fremont cottonwoods (*Populus fremontii*) and willows (*Salix* spp.) and occasionally the helleborine orchid (*Epipactis gigantea*).

When novelist Zane Grey visited Furnace Creek Wash in 1919, he wrote, "This stream

of warm water flowed down from a gully that headed up in the Funeral Mountains. It had a disagreeable taste, somewhat acrid and soapy. A green thicket of brush was indeed welcome to the eye. It consisted of a rank, coarse kind of grass, and arrowweed, mesquite, and tamarack [sic]. The last-named bore a pink fuzzy blossom, not unlike pussy-willow, which was quite fragrant."

Believing that they were "improving" the desert, pioneers, the CCC, and the national park service planted tamarisk. Unfortunately, it consumes excessive amounts of water and salinizes soils where its salty leaves fall, killing off competing plants. Two species occur in Death Valley National Park—saltcedar (*Tamarisk ramosissima*), a deciduous shrub from southern Asia, that produces thousands of seeds, and athel (*Tamarisk aphylla*), an evergreen tree native to northern Africa, whose seeds do not germinate. Since 1972, the park has been attempting to eradicate tamarisk.

Rock nettle.                    PHOTO© CAROL POLICH

Beavertail pricklypear.                    PHOTO© FRED HIRSCHMANN

Tamarisk.                    PHOTO© JEFF D. NICHOLAS

**PAGE 60/61:** *Rainbow over field of creosote bush, desert gold, and the Amargosa Range.* PHOTO© RANDI HIRSCHMANN

Sand verbena growing in profusion along 4-wheel-drive road.

# SURVIVING THE SUMMER

The left rear tire sinks in the soft dirt and no amount of rocking will dislodge the car. The temperature hovers around 110° F in the shade. The driver sets off to get help while his wife and young daughter sit in the shade of the stuck vehicle. The heat is oppressive. On and on he walks, the distant mountains coming no closer. His steps become leaden. He feels nauseous, his vision blurry. He doesn't notice the fork in the road. In the hazy distance, he thinks he sees a blue, shimmering lake with reedy shores where tiny white rowboats bob gently. Stumbling onward, the mirage melts away and all that remains is a burning white alkali flat over which heat waves dance dizzily. By now, he has totally forgotten about the canteen on his belt. Somehow he has lost his hat and shirt. He falls to his knees and convulses. His core temperature has risen to a deadly 106° Fahrenheit.

Later that day, a ranger on patrol discovers the traveler's baked and blistered body. Following the dead man's tracks in the dirt road, the ranger finds the stuck car and the wife and child—hot and parched but still alive.

**Play it safe**. Tell someone where you are going and when to expect you back. Don't rely on your cell phone; try dialing 911, but service is unreliable in the park. **Carry extra water** (at least 1 gallon per person per day) and plenty of gas and a shovel, especially if exploring back roads. Check on road conditions; many of the back roads are suitable only for rugged, high-clearance, four-wheel-drive vehicles. **Do not drive off designated roads** (this includes bicycles). Off-road travel not only injures fragile desert plants but leaves tracks that can remain for decades. **Closed vehicles make great ovens**; don't cook your children or pet. **Avoid the lower elevations during the summer months**; it's much cooler in the mountains. **Stay out of narrow canyons** and dry washes if there is any threat of rain. Flashfloods can arrive unannounced. **Stay out of mine tunnels**. Watch out for broken glass and sharp, rusty metal objects around historic sites.

Drink more than you think you need; **drink often**; eat a little salty food, too. **Wear light-colored clothing, a broad-brimmed hat, and sunglasses**. Potentially dangerous animals, such as rattlesnakes, scorpions or black widow spiders, can be easily avoided; watch where you place hands and feet. Basically, use common sense, plan ahead, and did I mention, **carry more water**?

## EMERGENCY & MEDICAL
24-HOUR EMERGENCY MEDICAL SERVICE
Dial 911

## ROAD CONDITIONS
ARIZONA          (888) 411-7623
CALIFORNIA       (800) 427-7623
NEVADA           (702) 486-3116

## MORE INFORMATION
DEATH VALLEY NATIONAL PARK
PO Box 579
Death Valley, CA 92328
(760) 786-3200
www.nps.gov/deva

DEATH VALLEY NATURAL HISTORY ASSOCIATION
PO Box 188
Death Valley, CA 92328
(760) 786-3285

NATIONAL PARKS ON THE INTERNET:
www.nps.gov

BUREAU OF LAND MANAGEMENT
www.blm.gov

CALIFORNIA DESERT INFORMATION
www.californiadesert.gov

## LODGING INSIDE THE PARK
FURNACE CREEK INN
(760) 786-2361 or www.furnacecreekresort.com
FURNACE CREEK RANCH
(760) 786-2345 or www.furnacecreekresort.com
PANAMINT SPRINGS RESORT
(775) 482-7680 or www.deathvalley.com
STOVEPIPE WELLS VILLAGE
(760) 786-2387

## CAMPING INSIDE THE PARK
Furnace Creek: (800) 365-CAMP (2267)
www.reservations.nps.gov
All other campgrounds are first come, first served.

## OTHER REGIONAL SITES
CALIFORNIA STATE PARKS
www.parks.ca.gov

NEVADA STATE PARKS
www.state.nv.us/stparks/

ANTELOPE VALLEY STATE POPPY RESERVE
15101 Lancaster Road
Lancaster, CA 93536
(661) 724-1180

ANZA BORREGO DESERT STATE PARK
Borrego Springs, CA 92004
(760) 767-5311

ASH MEADOWS NATIONAL WILDLIFE REFUGE
PO Box 115
Amargosa Valley, NV 89021
(775) 372-5435

BODIE STATE PARK
Bridgeport, CA 93517
(760) 647-6445

DEVILS POSTPILE NATIONAL MONUMENT
PO Box 3999
Mammoth Lakes, CA 93546
(760) 934-2289 (Summer), 872-4881 (Winter)
www.nps.gov/depo

JOSHUA TREE NATIONAL PARK
74485 National Park Drive
Twentynine Palms, CA 92277
(760) 367-5500
www.nps.gov/jotr

LAKE MEAD NATIONAL RECREATION AREA
601 Nevada Highway
Boulder City, NV 89005
(702) 293-8907
www.nps.gov/lame

MANZANAR NATIONAL HISTORIC SITE
PO Box 426
Independence, Ca 93526
(760) 878-2932
www.nps.gov/manz

MOJAVE NATIONAL PRESERVE
222 E. Main Street, Suite 202
Barstow, CA 92311
(760) 255-8801
www.nps.gov/moja

MONO LAKE TUFA STATE RESERVE
Lee Vining, CA 93541
(760) 647-6331

RED ROCK CANYON NATIONAL CONSERVATION
AREA
HCR 33, Box 5500
Las Vegas, NV 89124
(702) 363-1921

SEQUOIA/KINGS CANYON NATIONAL PARKS
Three Rivers, CA 93271
(559) 565-3341
www.nps.gov/seki

VALLEY OF FIRE STATE PARK
PO Box 515
Overton, NV 89040
(702) 397-2088

YOSEMITE NATIONAL PARK
PO Box 577
Yosemite National Park, CA 95389
(209) 372-0200, 372-4726 (TDD)
www.nps.gov/yose

## SUGGESTED READING
National Park Service. *A Walking Tour of Scotty's Castle.* Death Valley, CA: Death Valley Natural History Association. 2000.

Bryan, T. Scott and Betty Tucker-Bryan. *The Explorer's Guide to Death Valley National Park.* Niwot, CO: University Press of Colorado. 1995.

Collier, Michael. *An Introduction to the Geology of Death Valley.* Death Valley, CA: Death Valley Natural History Association. 1990.

Digonnet, Michel. *Hiking Death Valley: A Guide to its Natural Wonders and Mining Past.* Palo Alto, CA: published by the author. 1999.

Ferris, Roxana S. *Death Valley Wildflowers.* Death Valley, CA: Death Valley Natural History Association. 1983.

Houston, Eleanor. *Death Valley Scotty Told Me.* Death Valley, CA: Death Valley Natural History Association. 1985.

Johnson, Leroy and Jean Johnson. *Escape from Death Valley.* Reno & Las Vegas, NV: University of Nevada Press. 1987.

Kirk, Ruth. *Exploring Death Valley.* San Francisco, CA: Sierra Club Books. 1992.

Koenig, George. *Beyond This Place There Be Dragons: The Routes of the Tragic Trek of the Death Valley 1849ers through Nevada, DeathValley, and to Southern California.* Glendale, CA: Arthur H. Clark Company. 1984.

Lingenfelter, Richard E. *Death Valley & The Amargosa: A Land of Illusion.* Berkeley and Los Angeles, CA: University of California Press. 1986.

Lingenfelter, Richard E. and Richard A. Dwyer, editors. *Death Valley Lore: Classic Tales of Fantasy, Adventure, and Mystery.* Reno and Las Vegas, NV: University of Nevada Press. 1988.

Schoenherr, Allan A. *A Natural History of California.* Berkeley, CA: University of California Press. 1992.

Sharp, Robert P. and Allen F. Glazner. *Geology Underfoot in Death Valley and Owens Valley.* Missoula, MT: Mountain Press Publishing Company. 1997.

Weight, Harold O. *Twenty Mule Team Days in Death Valley.* Twentynine Palms, CA: Calico Press. 1955.

# PRODUCTION CREDITS

Publisher: Jeff D. Nicholas
Author: Stewart Aitchison
Editor: Nicky Leach
Production Assistant: Marcia Huskey
Illustrations: Darlece Cleveland
Printing Coordination: Sung In Printing America

ISBN 1-58071-041-7(Cloth), 1-58071-042-5(Paper)
©2002 Panorama International Productions, Inc.

## SIERRA PRESS

4988 Gold Leaf Drive, Mariposa, CA 95338
(209) 966-5071, 966-5073 (Fax)
e-mail: siepress@yosemite.net

SIERRA PRESS

**VISIT OUR WEBSITE AT:**
**www.nationalparksusa.com**

**BELOW**
Teakettle Junction. PHOTO© TERRY DONNELLY
**OPPOSITE**
Death Valley salt pan seen from Dantes View.
PHOTO© JEFF GNASS
**BACK COVER/FRONT COVER**
Sand dunes detail. PHOTO© DENNIS FLAHERTY
**BACK COVER** (TOP INSET)
Salt pan detail seen from Dantes View.
PHOTO© JEFF D. NICHOLAS
**BACK COVER** (MIDDLE INSET)
Joshua tree near Lee Flat. PHOTO© LARRY ULRICH
**BACK COVER** (BOTTOM INSET)
Lichen-covered volcanic rock and snakeweed.
PHOTO© JACK DYKINGA